# The Night
# We Danced
# With the Raelettes

## Occurrences In and Around College Park
## Maryland in the 1960s For the Most Part
## To the Best of My Recollection

# Charles Rossiter

*for Jeannine —*
*May the words be with you.*
*Charlie Ross[iter]*
*Nov 2008*

FootHills Publishing

## Acknowledgements

The Summer I Brought in the Yeast--*After Hours*
US 1 Ran Right Through Campus--*Shampoo (online literary magazine)*
When Someone Asks Me Who Was First, Bethlehem Steel, & Ah Nan. . .--*Paterson Literary Review*
The First Time the Library Saved My Life--*Rough Draft*
Coffeehouse Days--*Atelier*
Classics for a Quarter--*Depot Anthology*
Snow Blind in Nebraska--*Journal of Poetry Therapy*
Regret--*LIPS*

-------

*The following poems were included in the one-act, one-person play entitled *The Night We Danced With the Raelettes* produced at Victory Gardens Theater, Chicago--an experiment in poetry theater.

Into the Wide World
The Trash Can Cooler
When Someone Asks Me Who Was First
The Night the Rubber Broke
The First Time the Library Saved My Life
The Night I Slept in the Leaves
At the Ocean
The Night We Danced With the Raelettes

Cover Art and Design by Walter Negron

Back Cover photo by Bill DuPree

ISBN: 0-941053-28-8

FootHills Publishing
P. O. Box 68
Kanona, NY 14856
www.foothillspublishing.com

# Contents

# Introduction

Writing these poems reminded me of some of the differences
between life in the university then and now. Once things
change, it's sometimes hard to recall "the way we were." Lest
these little details of college life in the 60's be forgotten,
**here are just a few of the important differences.**

In the older section of campus where I lived, men and women
lived in separate dorms. When new high-rise dorms were built
on the back side of campus, men and women lived on different
floors.

Getting an abortion was a very big deal as well as illegal most
places. Couples sometimes got married because the girl got
pregnant.

The electric circuitry in the dorms couldn't support a lot of
appliances, or so we were told. The only television for the 70-80
guys in our dorm was in the basement lounge. As a result,
many just skipped it. Some groups made a weekly ritual of
watching particular shows--*The Untouchables* comes to mind.

There was one phone on each of our three floors. Someone
would answer if it rang and go get whoever was being called.
Guys did not like getting assigned the room nearest the phone.

Men and women were definitely not treated equally by the
housing office. The women had curfews. They signed out at
the front desk whenever they left the building and signed back
in when they returned. Guys had no hours and could come and
go as they pleased, unmonitered.

The doors to the men's dorm buildings were never locked.

Both men and women's dorms had "housemothers" who
inspected the rooms each week.

**On the other hand, some things remain the same. Like college students today. . .**

We were all trying to figure out what to do with our lives.

Love and sex figured big in our lives and thoughts..

Money was an issue for many of us who barely got by living the low-cashflow student existence.

Overall it was a beautiful time of life dedicated to learning and figuring out life, hanging with friends and talking late. One of the great losses of adulthood is the time to just be with friends, flopped around a room late at night talking about whatever comes up.

Charlie Rossiter, 2007

5

## Into the Wide World

I left my parents' house at 18
with all the worldly goods
that meant anything--
bongo drums, guitar,
tape recorder, records,
books, barbells, camera
and a few clothes
packed in a twenty year old Chevrolet
for an eighteen hundred mile drive
cross country
to my Nan's house
and a try at college.

no money to speak of
no connections
no knowledge
    of how the world works,
armed only with the urge to learn
and to not spend my days
sweating in factory death mills

I slept in the car at roadside rests
to save money for gas and peanut butter.
The trip took sixty hours.
In Kansas, thunderstorms
and roaring semis shook
my four-wheel lifeboat,
lightning streaked and crackled,
across the unearthly sky
to the far horizon, half a dozen
fingers of fire at a time as I lay
curled in my thin blanket
waterfalls of rain cascaded down
the windows.
The second day a friendly trucker
helped a dumb kid change a tire, offering
"you can't take long trips on those retreads"
but I plunged onward over steep

Alleghany mountain passes
that slowed me to 40
so that I needed to race
back up to 75 on the downhill side
to make it up the next mountain
and on into Maryland.  The third day
I arrived in Baltimore
like a homing pigeon miraculously
recognized landmarks
from years earlier
that led me home.

Waking past noon, rested
fed on Nan's scrambled eggs
the food of my childhood,
I spent the afternoon
unloading the car
into Uncle Fred's old bedroom.
Surveying the jumble
of my earthly belongings
I sat on the edge of
Uncle Fred's bed
shuddered
and said a little prayer.
I was scared
and I was happy.

The trip was over.
The journey was about to begin.

## The Trash Can Cooler

50 gallons
of galvenized steel
bought
with the dorm treasury
to take beer
to the drive-in.
The drive-in was
a buck a carload
so we needed something
large. We squeezed
6 or 7 guys in the car
and needed something
big enough
for at least
a couple cases
of National Bohemian.
Ice was no problem
a motel near campus
had a machine
around back.
The problem was
the can leaked
so the car stayed wet
for 3 or 4 days.
There was
also the issue of
sweat, a cold steel
trashcan builds up
a heap of condensation
on the outside
which didn't do much
for the guy
sitting next to it.

I think I mostly remember
that beautiful silver
trashcan
because it was. . .

more than a trashcan
it was a symbol
like the horseshoes
that clanked outside
our window
bought with dorm funds
and the ping pong table
in the basement
built by guys
in woodshop,
the tv in the lounge
bought for 10 bucks
at a 7 a.m.
Washington's Birthday sale
or even the dorm test file
in my roommate Fred's closet.
That trashcan testified
we were more than a
dorm full of strangers
we were by God
drinking buddies.

## Another Night With the Guys

Around midnight
Gene convinced us
to drive to Annapolis
where a friend of his
ran a pool hall.

"We'll play free
all night"

Four of us got in
Little Dave's rusty Studebaker
with a couple six packs
of Country Club Malt Liquor
and a fifth
of Old Grand Dad.
It was thirty miles
and snowing.
Before we hit the beltway
we were into
the Country Club.
By the time we reached
the pool hall
we were flying.

The place was empty
and of course
the friend had quit
a month before.
We shot a couple games
of eight ball
and in an hour
we were
out of there.
We'd finished the Country Club
but we still had
the Old Grand Dad
and four big plastic cups
from the pool hall.
We filled the cups

with roadside snow
and emptied the bottle
over them
to make bourbon
snowballs.

The thirty miles back
could have been a hundred
with snow coming down
and the Old Grand Dad,
but Little Dave was a genius
at the wheel
and brought us in
just as the sky
began to lighten.
Before we went inside
two of us threw up
in the parking lot.

Next morning
head throbbing,
I stood at the window
and wondered
what we thought
we were doing.
You could still see
the way the snow was different
beside Little Dave's car.
He'd parked across
two spaces
and one back door
was wide open.
It was another one of those
nights with the guys
when something
was supposed to happen
but nothing
really
did.

## Defiantly Undeclared

Engineering majors laughed at us
unable to comprehend
why we couldn't or wouldn't
pick a major and stick with it
the way we couldn't imagine
deciding at nineteen
not to explore what's out there
just to know.

Defiantly undeclared
we winced at the ridicule
but inside we knew,
we had been to Europe
we read Sartre and Camus
we tried new things
even if they didn't lead directly
to a job
or to anything
more than a little learning
about ourselves
and the world

We were few
but we were not alone.

When the catalog came out each year
we could feel the love
when the University PR boys
extolled the virtues of learning
and the liberal arts,
there we were
in all our unfocused glory,
much maligned,
unrepentant,
defiantly undeclared.

## She Was One of Those Scary Women

She had a plain face
kind of hang dog
but a cute enough little body
that she was willing
to use
and she gave
a good blow job.

The first time,
we were in the back seat
of my buddy Gordon's car
necking.
I put her hand there
and she
pulled it out
looked up at me and said
*what do you want?*
I said
*take a guess.*

Knowing what I know now
I'd say she had no self-esteem
at all.
She was like the bottom dog
in the pack
sniffing around
hoping to avoid rejection.
That blow job
brought me back
another time or two
but I got scared
and backed off.

Someone had hurt her
bad
and I didn't want to add
any more to that.

If I'd known what I know now
I'd have walked her
to the campus shrink
before she ended up
like one of those women
you read about
in the newspaper
walking down the middle
of US 1
in the dead of night
talking to herself
naked
and crying.

## Fred's First Beer

The night my roommate Fred
drank his first beer
and more at our urging
we were at a dorm party
in the back room
of a bar near campus,
a few bucks for all
you could drink.
A woman's dorm was there too
but we were freshmen
focused on the beer and Fred,
who after the third
began to ramble about life,
the dorm, and playing tuba
in the marching band.
After the fourth beer
he called the RA a pussy
to his face, something
Fred would never do in real life.
After the fifth beer
he put his head on the table
and closed his eyes.

He didn't throw up
until the night air hit him
as we led him to the car
to help him home
and tuck him in.
It was a rite of passage,
one more way to say welcome
to the fellowship of males.
I won't say men
because we were still boys
but we were working on it.

## Christmas Eve on The Block

She'd been a looker
you could tell
but she drew the short straw,
so that Christmas Eve
she was the only
stripper
in the house,
an old fashioned
burlesque
strip joint
held over from
the 40's.
Between costume changes
a guy in baggy pants
and plaid jacket
told old jokes
and sang
"Oh Suzanna"
while he played
the banjo.
The platform stage
was decorated
with a swag
of tinsel and
colored lights
and the audience,
all four of us,
sat in old wooden
theater chairs
bolted in rows
to the floor.
Every couple minutes
she stopped
after taking off
a glove
or necklace
or finally her
halter top,

and hustle
to the side of the stage
to turn over the
record
she was dancing to.

She still looked
good
but we could tell
she didn't ride
as high as she
used to,
standing there
twirling
her tassles
and touching her
toes
as the four of us
applauded
politely.
Then she bowed
slowly
like the Queen of Sheba
and walked off
the stage
carrying her costume
under one arm
with the record
she danced to
tucked up
under the other.

# The Summer I Brought in the Yeast

I was never into poker or hunting
or big league sports
but the summer I delivered yeast
for Budweiser I just about
felt like a good old boy.
All over DC in Dunkin Donuts,
Pizza Huts, corner bakeries
I brought in the yeast
and was greeted with
"hiya Charlie"
"what's happening?"
"how's it hanging?"
and other male bond talk.

Driving the Budweiser yeast truck I was
a guy among guys, a working stiff
among working stiffs, risking my ass
on jelly-greased cooler floors
of the Wonder Bread factory
where tubs of strawberry and grape jelly
sloshed over the edge of giant vats
the size of bathtubs
making the floor a skating rink
of reddish-hued sweetness and danger
over which I carried boxes filled
with one pound bricks of yeast
the size of gold bars stacked on palletes
in childhood movies of Fort Knox.

It didn't last of course.  I was
a substitute yeast man, standing in
for the regular good old boy
who was on vacation.   So when
the three weeks were up, I left
back to my soft life
of women and books,
music and sunsets.

On the last day
I turned in my truck keys
and bought three cases
with my employee discount.
They lasted a month.
I never drank Budweiser
again.

## U.S. 1 Ran Right Through Campus

On nights when I felt low
I stared out the window
at passing cars
and thought about how
that road
was a long straight shot
to Florida
if I had the nerve
to take it.

Guys I'd known
had disappeared there
into the world of work
cars and money,
a world without term papers
or blue books.
One guy came back
after a semester
with tales of big bucks
working as a bellhop
at a fancy hotel
in Miami. At the time,
that sounded good to me.
I was tired of that helpless
student feeling,
tired of counting pennies.
I was young and strong
and optimistic
that my life would be
beautiful
no matter what I did.

For months I wavered.

Classes were a drag
but I loved the library
the lectures

the National Symphony
on Tuesday nights.

It was nip and tuck there
for a while
between cutting out
and hanging on.
Then I met Nanya
and fell in love.
It was a grand passionate love
the kind filled
with continual fulfillments.

You know the rest.
She changed my life.
U.S. 1 became irrelevant,
I hung on.

## At the Kentucky State Fair

We drove a half-thousand miles
through Appalachian highlands
to run the midway dime toss
where we planned to make big bucks
through slight-of-hand
skimming coins
that missed the bright red
Lucky Strike circle,
ten for the boss, one for us
ten for the boss, one for us

The World's Largest Horse
stood tied to a trailer
behind the joint
we flashed each morning
with pink and aqua bunnies
three feet tall,
it's do or die
at the dime toss,
none of that
two out of three,
and you win big
stuff that takes two hands
to carry
and brings in
the losers
like us
in over our heads

Unprepared
for the boss's gun
and the mobsters behind him
we slaved twelve hour days
failed as Jesse James
and barely skimmed enough
to pay the motel.
Two days into

our life of crime
sick with heat and hustle
we threw in the towel
to wire-muscled carnies
and tattooed ladies,
dragged on home
to count our losings
lick our wounds
and plan our bets
for future dreams.

## MWF in the Armory

We social danced
in ways we never danced
in real life
tango, waltz, rhumba.
It was a PE class
and so we learned. . .
that girls can't dance
any better than guys,
they just practice more.

When we started together
on a set of moves
they were as klutzy
as we were.

The teacher
was straight out of
a Jules Pfeiffer
Village Voice cartoon
in black leotards
and long loose skirts,
also black,
the kind
modern dancers wear,
and long dark straight hair,
sexy
it seemed to me.
Despite being skinny
she could move,
and when she led
those girls
around the floor
she was a joy
to watch.
She only danced with girls
except
on rare occasions

when she
didn't want to lead
which gave the class
those days
an extra edge or maybe
that was just me.

She was picky about
male partners;
there were only
a few of us
she was willing
to follow
and none of us knew
what to make of that

I was too young
to care.
She was lithe
and strong
and her narrow waist
fit perfectly
in the curved palm
of my hand.

## When Someone Asks Me Who Was First

We still lived in dorms
segregated by sex
but I lived on the first floor
in back
which meant that
once we decided
it was easy
to lift her through the window
walk around
and come in the front door
as if nothing monumental
were about to happen
but it did
right there
in my narrow iron dorm bed
just a wall away
from the distant din
of rowdy dorm guys
without dates
on saturday night.

When someone asks me
who was first
I think of Nanya
and that night
which is not precisely true.
There was someone or two
before her, I'm almost certain.
I forget the details
and the names.

But the night I lifted
Nanya through the window
as if she were
a princess, Lady Guenivere,
Rapunsel-in-Reverse,
and I were Galahad

or Robin Hood
or any stirring figure
out of myth or legend.

That night
she became the first.

## The Night the Rubber Broke

I was making love
to the love
of my young life,
the night the rubber
broke.
It was a Trojan
lubricated
and till then
we'd always had faith
in Trojans.
We also watched the calendar;
we were determined
not to spoil the fun.

The calendar was
a little vague that night,
when the rubber broke
it mattered
so much
I wrote a letter
to the Young's Rubber Company
detailing my past faith
in their products,
now shattered
by the broken rubber.

I didn't expect a response
so I was surprised
the night the regional sales rep
appeared at my dorm room door,
an average looking guy
in a trenchcoat
with a salesman's briefcase.
He asked if I was the guy
who wrote the letter.

He had the letter in the briefcase.

I told him yeah
that's me
and I told him again
how under ideal conditions,
a perfectly normal roll in the hay
with my exquisitely lubricated
girlfriend,
their product had failed.

There's no excuse for that
he assured me
he was sorry for the failure
and that the company
takes these things
seriously.
He gave me a pack of rubbers
from the briefcase.
apologized again
and promised to send me
a sample pack
of their complete line.

The sample pack never came
which seemed odd
as they'd bothered
to send someone
in the first place,
but I didn't mind.
My girl had had her period,
we were still going at it
strong
and when word got out
that the Trojan guy
had paid me a personal visit
my status around the dorm
quickly rose
to something
just a shade short
of legendary.

## Ah Nan. . .

I can still see you
in your grandma flowered dress
sipping coffee by the window
in your chair by the radiator
as we talked and I ate
the scrambled eggs you fixed,
wash already on the line outside
the first loads done before I woke.

Your house on Washington Boulevard
was my growing up house
my stability, my rock.
You were there when I needed a haven.

It was you, Nan, who made my PB&Js
to eat while we watched Lucy
on Monday nights,
or played Pokeno with Blumey
on the porch next door.

It was in my college days
I discovered you would do anything for me
even bend your strict moral code
and look the other way,
especially look the other way,
I found that out when a pair of panties
that was not yours
turned up in the wash.

You showed them to me without flinching,
or threatening to kill me, and simply said:
"these must belong to your roommate Fred"
and we both knew you knew Fred was not a guy
who wore women's panties.

You never mentioned it again, and after that
Nanya and I were careful to check
that she went home with everything she came with

when you were away for the weekend
at Uncle Jimmy's.

Ah Nan. . .

I wish you could be here now so we could sit
on the porch and talk about nothing
the way we did in the old days. I wish we could
teach Jack all the old card games
starting with canasta. I wish you
could make us a couple of PB&Js,
but I know that's not going to happen.

You've been dead for twenty years
and I can accept that
because I learned from you,
from all those times you told me
when I wanted something
I wasn't going to get
*folks in hell want ice water*
and that's just the way it is.

## The First Time the Library Saved My Life

The first time
the library saved my life
was when my college girlfriend and I
broke up.
It was a crisp clear autumn day
full of gloom
and it drove me straight to the
one-forty's
for consolation.
I pulled out something
that read
like Wittgenstein,
so heady it turned
into a blur
of words,
but just being there
was familiar
and consoling.
Philosophy was on the top floor
in the back
where we used to meet and sweat
together,
this was before they
air-conditioned.

After a while up there
feeling sorry for myself
among the deep
thinkers
I started to believe
I could hear the building
breathing
but of course it was only
the ghosts of all those
philosophers asking questions
like *why?* and *what?* and
*how do you know?*
which was more disturbing
than consoling.

It was the longest afternoon
of my life
but I got through it
somehow
with my love of the library
untarnished
and only
a slight aversion
to Wittgenstein.

## You Were Brave Jim Dixon,
## Jim Dixon You Were Brave

The radio played blowing in the wind,
Stokely and Malcolm
gave speeches
and the farmers
on the Eastern Shore
got scared
they'd lose their cheap help
because the times
they were a changing

in the cities
the cops used guns
clubs, and baseball bats,

firehose stories
on the evening news

and through it all
you were brave
Jim Dixon,
the only black guy
in a dorm
with too many
eastern shore racists
who had the nerve
one night
to tape something
to your door
and burn it for kicks.

The University
let the scorch mark
stay there
till semester's end.

I felt for you Jim Dixon
but you were quiet,
kept to yourself,

and I didn't know enough
to knock on your charred door
to tell you
you were not
alone.

I felt for you Jim Dixon
but it took
a few more years
before I became a
take-it-to-the-streets
kind of guy.

That summer
driving to Ocean City
Mike and I
were stopped by roadblocks
on U.S. 50.
They were looking for shotguns
and "outside agitators,"
but they waved us by
without a second glance.
The only thing
we hoped to agitate
was hanging
between our legs,
and we weren't "carrying"
unless you count
a change of clothes
a couple towels
and a cooler full of
Pabst Blue Ribbon
beer.

## The Night I Slept in the Leaves

The idea was
to spend the night outdoors
and wake cleansed
of soul sickness
tests, deadlines,
cleansed
from the cramped feeling
of day in, day out

It was a great plan    but
have you ever slept in the leaves?

I woke at three
stiff, damp, cold
disheartened.
There was a lot of dew
in those leaves.

Cursing my stupidity
I stumbled inside
to bed.

Looking back
I could see
I was not
completely stupid.
I was wrong
about the comfort
of leaves
but I needed something
out of the ordinary
that night.
The leaves
didn't match my fantasy,
but that morning
I did feel a little bit
cleansed.

## At the Ocean

off-season midweek
on the empty beach
rereading *On the Road*
bummed out, lonely,
just out of love
my wreck of a car
up on blocks

a half-dozen stooped men
with sharp sticks
and cotton field gunny sacks
shuffled past
behind a rusted
city dump truck
picking up beach trash

one of them, about my age
looked over and waved.
I waved back

*You got it made* he called
in my direction
and bent back
to his picking

wham!

his words like lightning
lit the landscape
I saw clearly
beads of sweat
that dripped down
his tired face
into the sand,
glimpsed briefly
his likely future. . .
and mine. . .

*Maybe I do have it made*
    I thought
            *maybe I do*

## Classics for a Quarter

It was a ramshackle place by the tracks
run by a mother and son,
a place of homemade bookshelves,
yellowed cartoons
and faded photographs,
completely idiosyncratic
as good used bookstores are
and blessed with the sweet fragrance
of old books

        It was a short stroll
from the basement apartment
to an endless supply of Steinbeck
Caldwell, Miller, Burroughs,
Kafka, Dos Passos, Kerouac

classics for a quarter

I spent long hours there
on warm afternoons
browsing the world
of words
I was just beginning to learn,
chatting with the owner
about which author moved me
which new passion
to take home

The Old Riverdale Bookstore
is closed now, all traces gone,
but some of those fragile first tomes
still stand on my shelves.

Quiet nights alone
I take them down     gently
turn their weathered pages,
remind myself
who I was
who I am

breathe them in.

## Coffeehouse Days

At the Magpie in D.C.
we drank espresso, and discussed
Rimbaud, zen and Celine,
heard hip black poets do Ferlinghetti
to a bop piano
and tried to know time.

America was too clean for us,
we craved the weird beauty of dirt
so we wore black berets and dreamed
of Tangiers, Mexico, drank
cheap wine and sweat it out
imagining blood.

Summer nights in cramped cars,
on park benches, under boardwalks
with strangers or friends.
How you slept mattered
back then. At home
the mattress was on the floor.

## Snow Blind in Nebraska

The light was blinding white
from oncoming headlights
and our own
reflected back
as I pushed it at fifty
driving through the night
radio tuned to K-O-M-A
across the flatlands
of Nebraska
from the coast
to Colorado
for a long weekend
with my buddy Craig.

Around two, Mike woke
in the back seat
and almost yelled out in terror,
snow blind,
he later told me,
but just then
guys being guys
all he said was,

*how's it going?*

and crawled
into the front seat
to keep me company
and awake
as we plowed through
the prairie night,
hearts set
on adventure,
the mountains,
the coming dawn.

## Regret

She was sweet
and she was right
I was a horny bastard
but she
responded to my kisses
and moved past
her ambivalence
to something like
desire.

I knew
she'd had a long-time steady
and she was ready
for what came next
            and next. . .

Her ass
was like fine silk,
there was a thick bush
I recall
a forest of desire
as in an ancient fairy tale
I plunged into her darkness.

My reward, the moment.
She refused to see me
when I called,
a victim of the old cliche
*you might get what you think you want*

She made it clear
I'd made my bet and lost,
a bit of short term bliss
inside her then
against the chance
to try to win her heart.

## The Last Time I Ever Had Roommates

The last time I ever had roommates
we lived in this basement apartment
with just a kitchen
and one big bedroom
with four beds.

There were three of us.

The couch was in the kitchen.
It was the back seat
of an old Ford Falcon.
The sink was a tub
the washing machine
would have drained into
if we'd had
a washing machine.
The refrigerator was
one of those little ones,
executives have
in their offices,
and the stove had only
two working burners.

I don't remember much
of what we did there
except get laid
in that extra fourth bed
nobody slept in
and drink Pabst Blue Ribbon.

There was always a Pabst
on hand
because the corner grocery
about a hundred yards
down the railroad tracks
just outside the back door,
our only door,
had a permanent sale
on Pabst Blue Ribbon Beer.

We bought it
in long neck returnables
for three bucks a case.
Then two of us
would each take an end
and carry it home
along the tracks.
If we had extra money
we'd splurge
on a big bag of chips
and call it a party.

Years later
I returned to the old place
but the house had been torn down
and the street
with the little corner grocery
had been re-routed,
but the tracks were
still there.
So I found a liquor store
and bought a six pack
of Pabst Blue Ribbon
and a big bag of chips
and sat down on the tracks
to raised a toast
to my buddies
Little Dave and Big John
and to the girl
who fucked me
senseless
in the bed nobody slept in,
then I grabbed
a handful of chips
took a swig
of Pabst Blue Ribbon
and called it
a party.

## The Strawberry Patch

I was a guide
at the pick-your-own
strawberry patch
with a pith helmet
that kept me thinking "straw boss"
and picturing the pickers
as convicts in an old
down south
prison farm movie

The customers were
out on a lark picking
and my only job was to lead them
to an empty row and
if they strayed from the row
to urge them back.
No one wants to crawl
a row of strawberry plants
behind someone who
just picked it.

It was a good system
but sometimes I'd get
a rambunctious old lady
who knew damn well
we wouldn't stop her
from slipping over a couple rows
to pick a few choice ones.
The worst offenders
were three old ladies
in their seventies
who absolutely would not
stay in their rows.
As they picked and rambled
I cajoled them back
as they told stories.

One had been Miss Alaska
back in her 20's

*Oh she was a looker.*
*All the men wanted her.*
*She was the queen*
*of all the parades*
*and rode in the biggest convertibles*
*wearing a swim suit*

She'd lived with a gold miner
until she got fed up
with his drinking
and ran away to San Francisco.
Another raised earthworms
in her highrise apartment
to sell to fishermen.

*You should see her kitchen.*
*It's full of worms.*
*I don't know how she can stand it.*

We passed a couple hours that way
with me chasing them back
in their own rows
and prodding the stories along.
I would have stayed
in that patch all summer
listening to life tales,
but the strawberry season
is a short one
and I was hired near the end.
After three days
the boss paid me off,
I packed up my pith helmet
and moved on to a new job
as a part-time Good Humor Man.

## Bethlehem Steel

Long sleeved shirts, steel-toed boots,
protective glasses and hard hat in
summertime Baltimore 100 humid degrees
walking the edge of coal fields where
buckets take two ton bites to move coal
from barge or train car to great bins or
conveyors where it travels up and
over to other belts and finally into
blast furnaces that make the steel.
Showering sparks and workmen
shadowed by molten metal look
heroic on tv screens but what
the camera never shows is
sulphur stench and acid burns,
hands flattened in train car
couplings, broken bones
from crane falls, death by crushing
when someone forgets for a moment
and goes down between barge
and pier, friday night
parking lot six-packs and fights
at neighborhood carry-outs
that cash the paychecks, the way
coal dust won't wash out and
most men's wives make them
burn the clothes.

## Peanut Butter Sandwiches
## Without Jelly

It was near the end of summer
and I was tired
of working the steel mill
and scared as well.
Looking down
at my fingers
I counted
ten
and told the boss
I quit.
The next day
Mike and I
left
for Daytona.

We were not thinking
hurricane

but. . .

for three days
we ate oatmeal
and peanut butter
sandwiches
on the floor
of the Mainland
middle school gym,
for three days
palm trees
bent over
in rain and wind,
waves crashed
over piers
and houses,
for three days
we slept on the floor
of the Mainland

middle school gym
as the storm roared
up the coast
holding us tight.
We stayed up late,
read,
sang songs,
played chess
and ate
peanut butter sandwiches
without jelly,
oatmeal
without milk,
watched ourselves
stretched out
on the floor
of the Mainland
middle school gym,
our half-minute
of fame,
each night
on network news.

## It Was 95 Degrees and a Million Percent Humidity

I was poor and needed wheels
to get to my job
at the Post Office
so I bought this
10-year-old tinny
little French car SIMCA
for two hundred bucks.
It ran all right
for about a month
then the troubles
began--
leaking oil,
burned out this and that.
I kept it patched together,
but the bills
were killing me.
Then one day--
it was 95 degrees
and a million percent humidity--
the way it gets
in DC summers,
I was at a stop sign
when this character
in a big air conditioned car,
this was before a/c was common,
hit me from behind,
not enough to hurt me
but enough
to push in the trunk
of the SIMCA.

As we stood there
in the blazing sun
the first thing he said was
"man it sure is hot"
loosening his tie
and I thought
"welcome to the world."

Then he said
"why'd you stop?"

I was young but I knew
a thing or two.
He hit me from behind
and he was going to pay.

All I said was "stop sign."

The cop arrived
took down the stop sign facts,
and we "exchanged information."
The SIMCA still drove
so I tied down the trunk
and went home.
Two weeks later
I got the check
for three hundred bucks.

The SIMCA was
officially totalled
but it limped on through
to the end of summer.
I sold it for fifty bucks
to a guy who knew cars.
I wished him
luck and figured
the SIMCA
had worked out pretty well
as a first serious brush
with capitalism
and the law.

## I Looked Like a Real Mailman

The truck was government issue white
with red and blue trim
and I wore a US Postal Service hat.
With that hat
and my mailbox keys
on a long chain
from my belt loop
I looked like a real mailmen.

My routes covered
some bad sections of DC,
out in Southeast
but I was lucky.
None of the gangs bothered me
and I never dealt with dogshit
or other strange items
some of the guys found
in their boxes.
All I did was drive around
and pick up mail,
stuff it into big gray canvas bags,
and drive it down to headquarters.

The only thing wrong
with the job
was that it took an hour
to get downtown
and the route I ran
took two and a half hours
so I was blowing
half the day
for only a couple hours pay.

I was a substitute
covering routes for guys
who were on vacation.
Who knew how long
the route was supposed
to take a rookie.

I started killing time
to see how far
I could stretch it.
Every afternoon .
I pulled into
the New York Avenue
McDonalds for a
a Big Mac and a coke.
If a supervisor came by
I planned to tell him
I got hungry.

The supervisor never came

so every day
I sat at McDonalds
for an hour or so
to eat and read.

I was reading
Henry Miller's *Tropic of Cancer.*
His ravings about
how hard it is
to live for art
with no money,
and his adventures
with loose women
all over Paris,
along with my
good paying
Post Office job
made it
one of the best summers
ever.

## The Night We Danced With the Raelettes

We heard about it from Fat Daddy
between a couple
of Bobby Blue Bland sides
on WSID.
It was a dance
sponsored by the King Street Social Club
and Ray Charles was the band.

We knew the music
we knew S I D
we knew the neighborhood
we drove to for the tickets,
but we still were not prepared
for the line
that stretched around the building
when we arrived
to be 100%
non-caucasian.
This was
a once-in-a-lifetime night.

We got in line.

Across the street
we saw two girls
looking over with curious
and very hesitant expressions
on their young white faces.
Feeling supremely cool
for being there ourselves
we called them over, talked them up
and they stayed.

The Armory was arranged
church social style, long rows
of folding tables with white
table clothes, each with a huge
bowl of ice surrounded by mixers,
chips and other snacks.

It was BYO and our O was a fifth
of Old Grand Dad.  The tables
stretched from dance floor
to building's edge, in a starburst
from the center stage.

The first dance we grabbed the girls
and hit the floor.  Half-way through
two guys cut in.
Then two guys cut in on them.
Mike and I could see
where this was heading so
we began cutting in ourselves.
The band played furiously,
Ray had an edge
to everything he touched in those
early days.  We worked through
a half-dozen numbers and twenty
or thirty partners
till our shirts were drenched.

Back at the table
we introduced ourselves
and started talking music.
Someone was related to a Shirelle,
someone else
grew up with Little Anthony.
Everyone knew someone
whose music we loved.
At some point
Mike tottered off
with the Old Grand Dad,
the girls went off dancing
and I was left talking to a
beautiful woman in a low cut
red dress.
Ray Charles was blasting, but
all my twenty-year old mind could hear
was an old Howling Wolf tune

about a long tall woman
they all called the chocolate drop.

When Mike came back
he was all smiles.
He'd been dancing
with a Raelette's cousin
and had joined them at their table.

The rest of the night flew by
in a haze of bourbon and blues,
red dresses and Raelettes.
The girls we met outside left early.
We stayed till the end
till the last notes faded
till the cleaning crew appeared
and began to sweep up
till the last revelers shuffled
zombie-like to the doors.

Driving home in Mike's re-wired old Ford
Fat Daddy was doing the late show,
James Brown was screaming "Try Me,"
the moon was up
and Baltimore never looked so good.

## Looking Back

We were not trained professionals
on a closed course;
our lives were an open road
and we were in a state
where the rules were vague.

It's a wonder anybody made it
casting about as we were,
in a mass of youthful hormones
and thrashing energy
searching for direction,
learning together
how to avoid dangerous curves
how to get around the roadblocks,
how to survive
long hellish nights in the world
and arrive home still breathing.

It took so many bad decisions
and foolhardy trials
crossing the lines
to find the lines
and more willpower
than many of us had
to do the right thing
once we found them.